TRACE LETTERS WORKBOOK GRADES PRESCHOOL
Children's Reading & Writing Education Books

All Rights reserved. No part of this book may be reproduced or used in any way or form or by any means whether electronic or mechanical, this means that you cannot record or photocopy any material ideas or tips that are provided in this book

Copyright 2016

Trace the letters with a pencil.

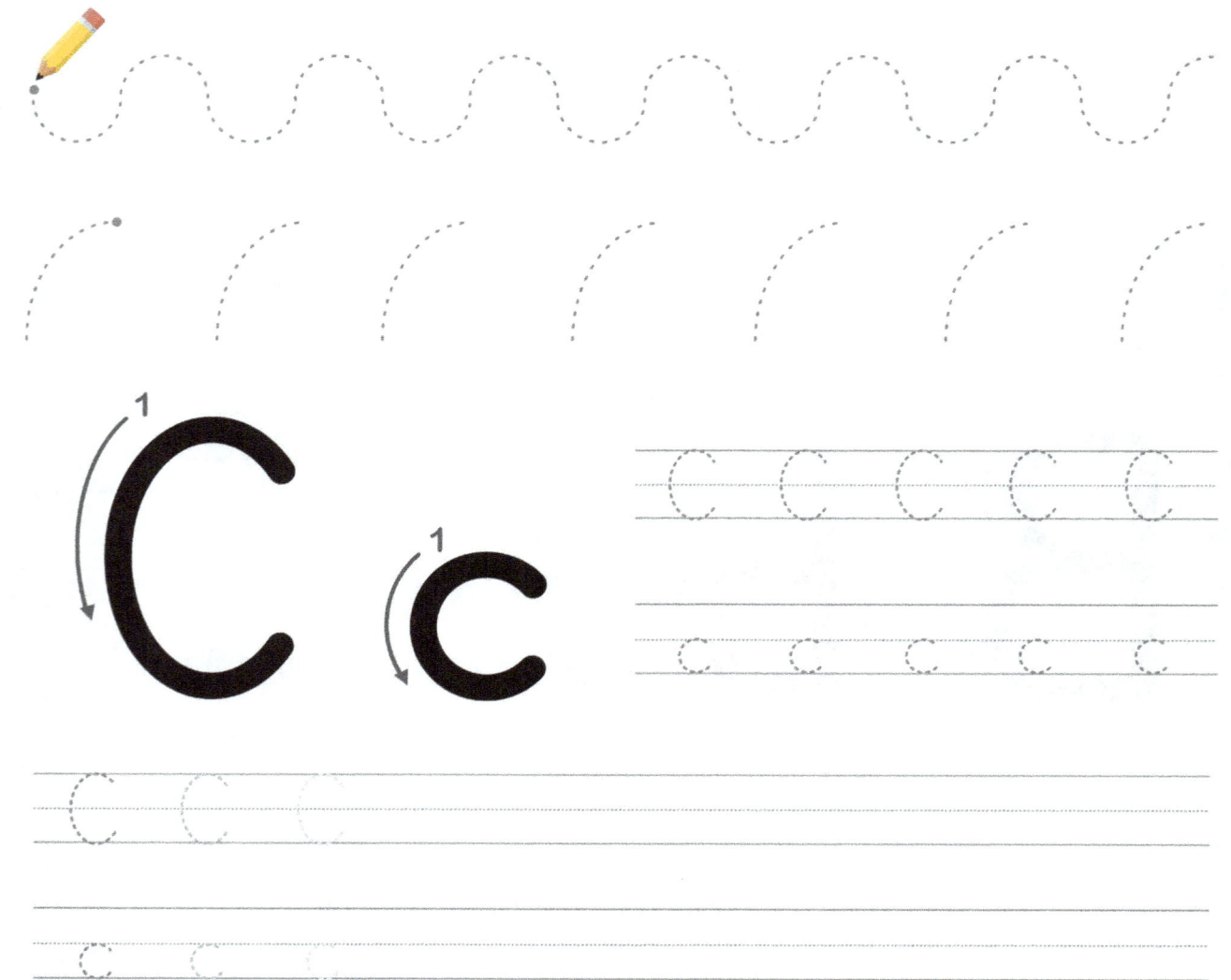

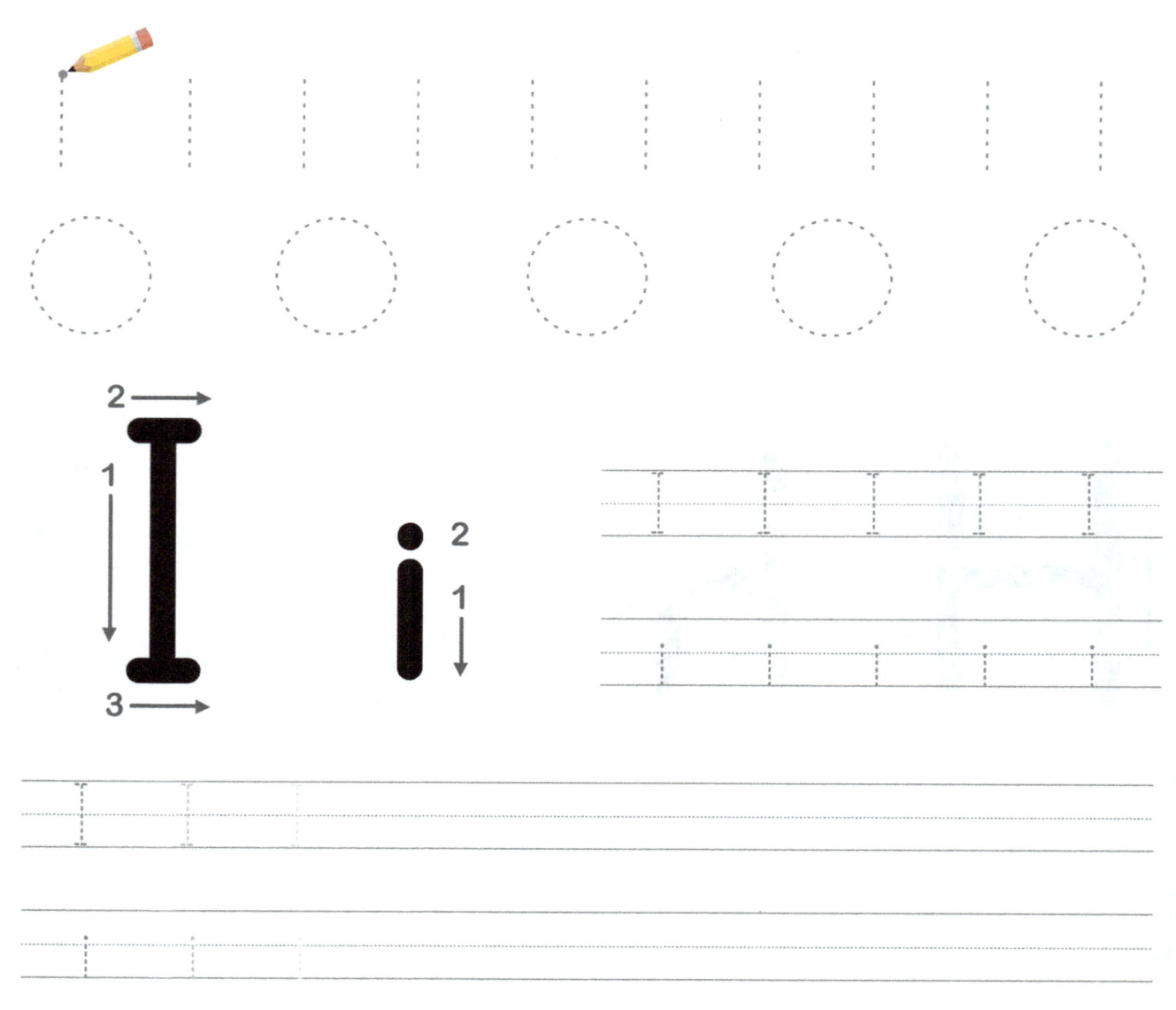

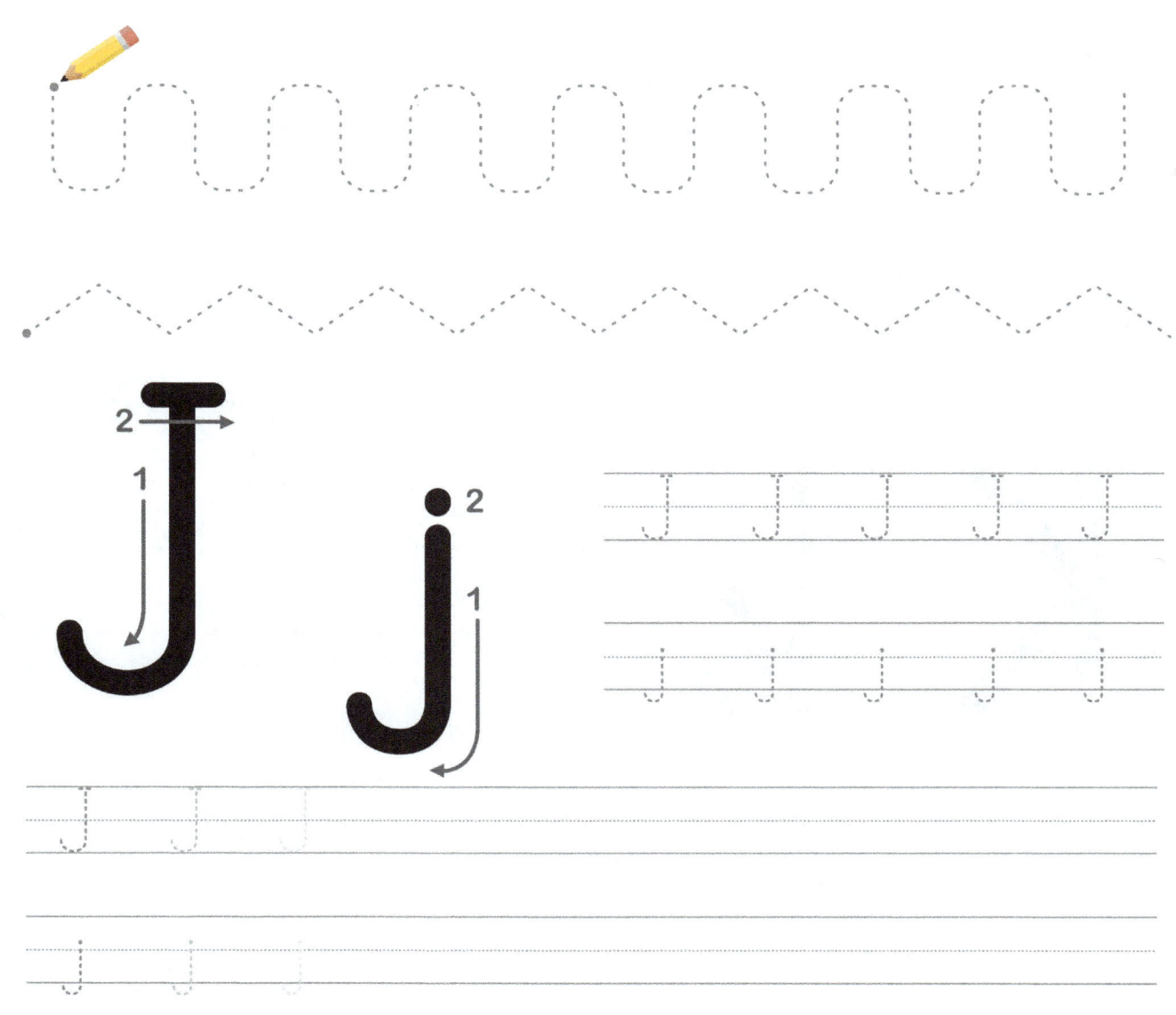

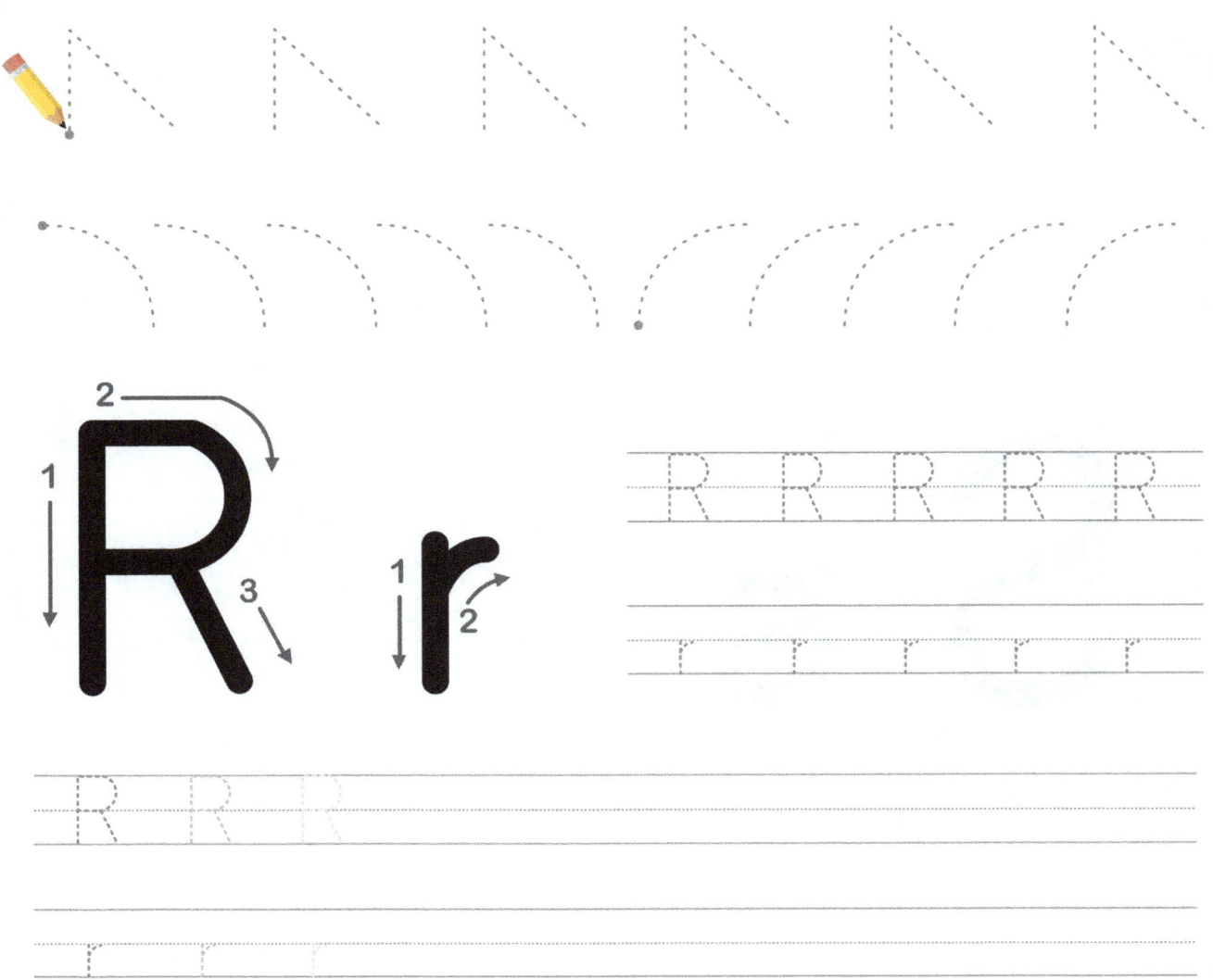

Trace the words with a pencil.

word

list

name

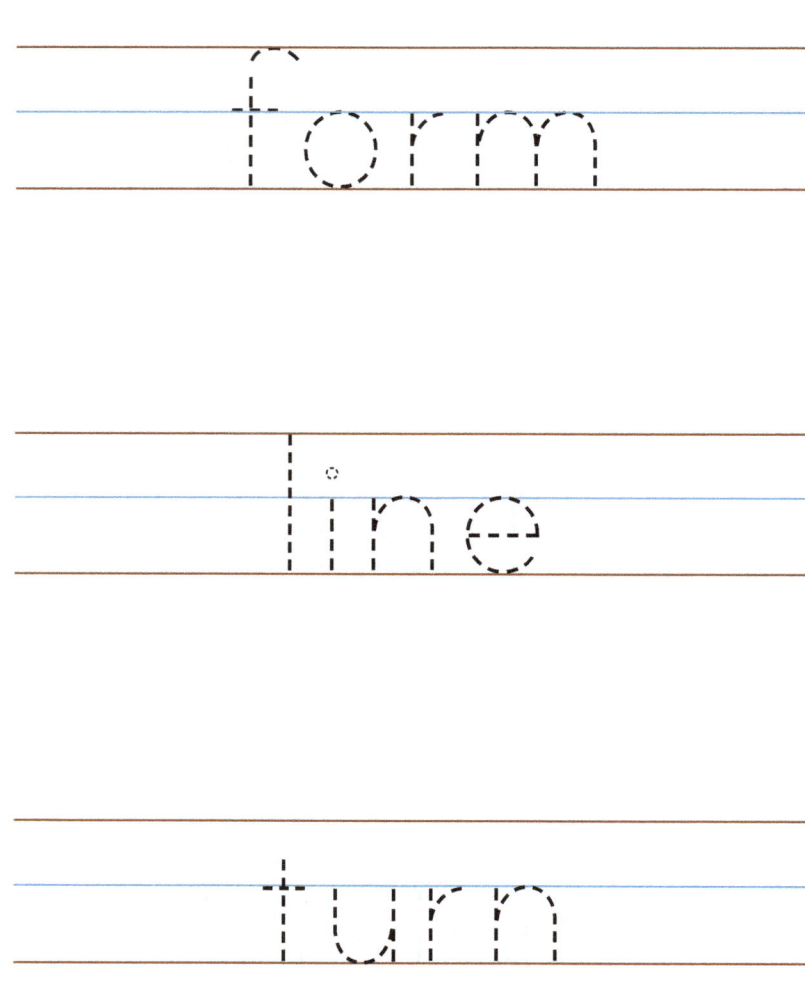

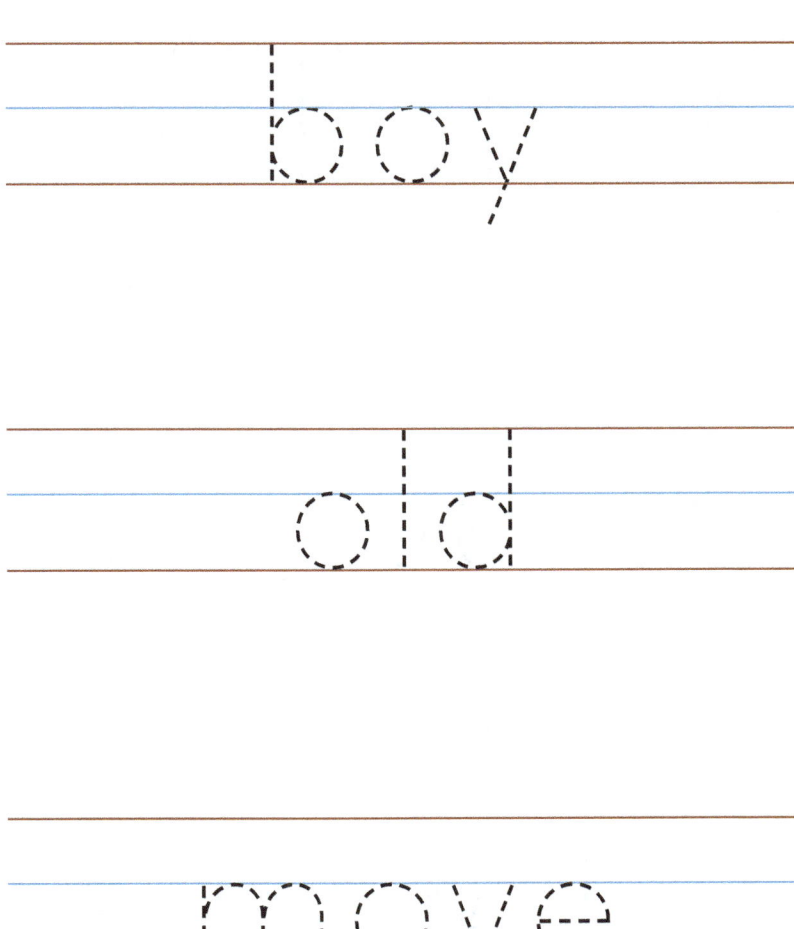

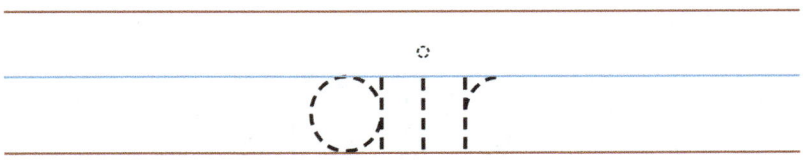

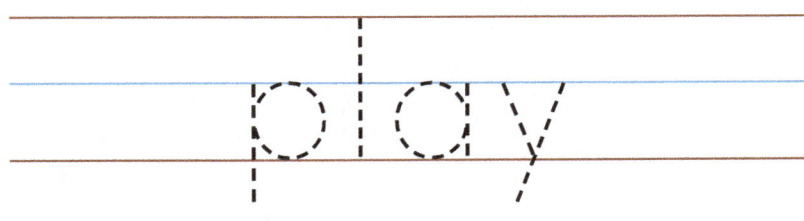

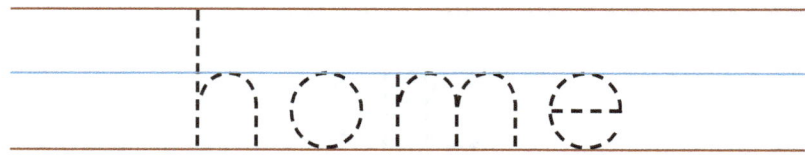

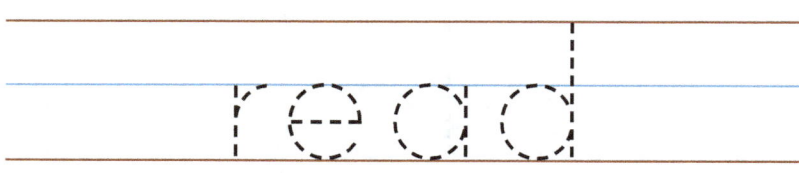

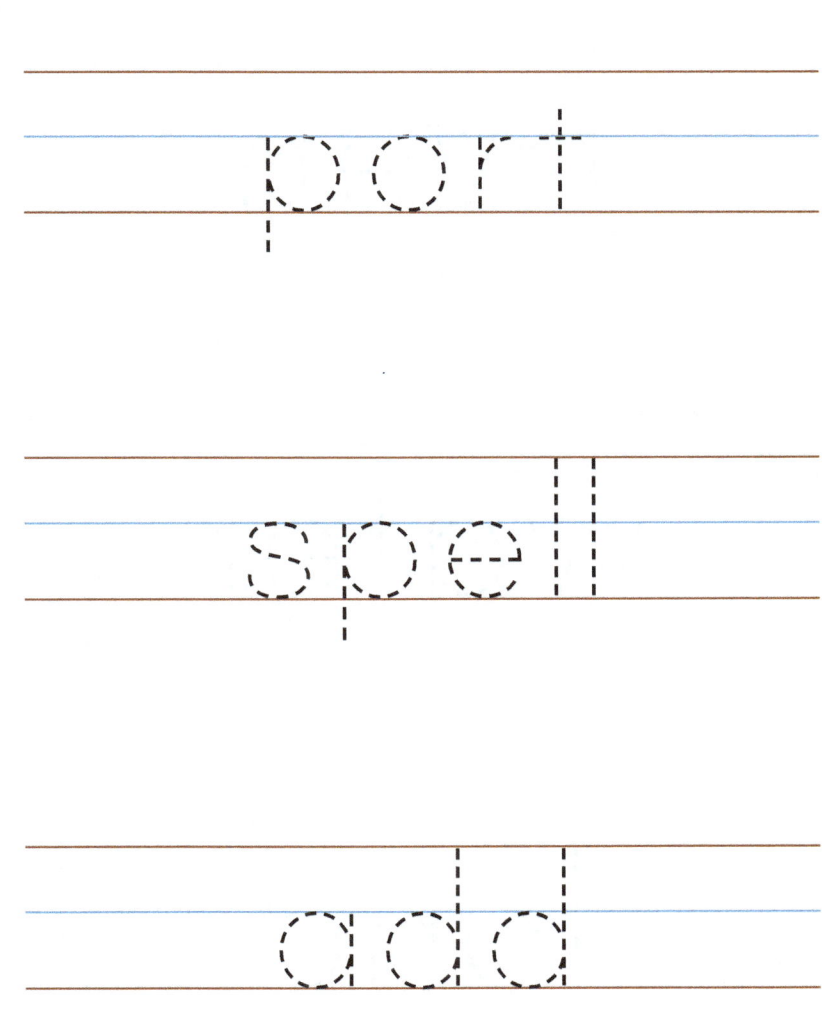

even

water

land

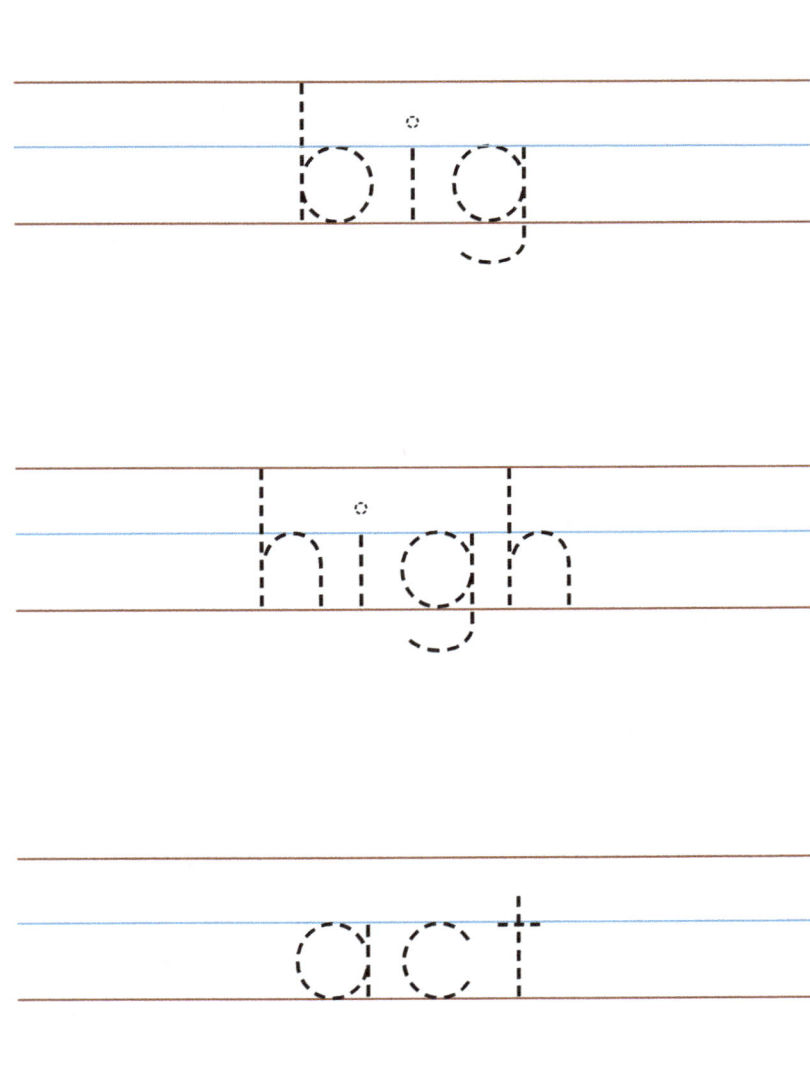

www.ingramcontent.com/pod-product-compliance
Lightning Source LLC
LaVergne TN
LVHW061325060426
835507LV00019B/2296